Beyond Me

Nin Reckermann

BookLeaf Publishing

India | USA | UK

Presentation by *BookLeaf Publishing*

Web: www.bookleafpub.com

E-mail: info@bookleafpub.com

ISBN: 978-93-5744-950-2

First edition 2022

DEDICATION

To everyone who has touched my life in such a way that I had no other choice but to write another poem.

ACKNOWLEDGEMENT

Thank you Mathilda for telling me about this opportunity.

PREFACE

Content Warnings:
Page 4: graphic death
Page 6: depression
Page 16: scars

Every Day

9. October 2021, 18:45

Every day can be deciding
Can incite your glorious ark
If you just come out of hiding
Out of cover, out of dark
If you trust your own hands' action
Trust your lips in every deed
Every train can be your traction
Every grain bright future's seed

Bewitched

11. October 2021, 01:00

you've moved into my mind and now
you occupy it whole
bewitched, enchanted, hexed somehow
my body and my soul
but if I kissed you would it wake
a feeling I now fear
or would the action shatter, break
this love I hold so dear

Autumn evening
12. October 2021, 20:47

took a step into the ev'ning
yellow streetlights, leaves that drip
autumn crystallized my breathing
froze my fingers, dried my lip
yet I smile into the darkness
as the cold my nose tip numbs
in unpleasantness my lark is
thoughts of you warm up my lungs

Prey

13. October 2021, 23:07

You pray to those who prey on you
In hopes you'll be like them
The ropes you lay to reach the view
Are those from which you'll hang

Gentle hand
14. October 2021, 23:55

Did you mean to be so tender
Gentle hand on lower back
Did you mean for it to render
Me, so delicate, a wreck
I leaned back and you leaned forward
Chin on shoulder – resting place
If I wasn't such a coward
Would have turned to meet your face
What would have been your expression
What my feeling, what my fear
Would my act have caused depression
Would my stupor be more clear?

I no longer dread the Darkness

15. October 2021, 23:05

I no longer dread the darkness
I just let it come and roll
Play its usual charade
I let it sink and take its toll
'Stead of dread, a tired welcome
"You again? Well, go ahead"
Like you deal with autumn ending
And with the time you go to bed
'Tis a thing that has its placement
In the rhythm of my life
I simply let it take me over
Do not rise to stand in strife
This might sound, to you, depressing
Reading this might strain or sting
But remember, dear, the morning,
The returning of the spring

When I'm gone
16. October 2021, 00:10

When, carved in stone, they claim I'm gone
My dear, please keep me living
For words and stories carry on
And knowledge keeps on giving
My breath replaced by readers' lips
Reciting words I've written
My heart beats steady on the tips
Of tongues that ride my rhythm

Friend
16. October 2021, 20:40

I want to call you, dear, my "friend"
With the intensity of "lover"
I want the word itself to send
A care so deep that it will hover
Right between your ribs and heart
So lips will start what never end
Will never break apart

Why is it that a friend is less
In many people's thinking
When really it is them that best
Do keep my boat from sinking
A friend like you are one I'd e'er
Prefer o'er romance' mess
For you will always care

Wonders of my World

17. October 2021, 01:10

Praise be with the ones beside me
Praise with you, my closest friends
Cannot put in words the many
Joys your presence through me sends
When with you, e'en gloom feels golden
When with you, my soul feels heard
I'm eternally beholden
To you, the wonders of my world

Pause –
17. October 2021, 02:00

Pause –
And hold on to this moment
Pause –
And take it in
Happiness like this is potent
Healing from within
Close your eyes
And feel it linger
Let your sighs reign free
Thank the life and thank its bringer
Whoever it may be

Seven of Stone
19. October 2021, 19:25

Oh, notes of grandeur
Tunes of adventure
Sounds that I can't bear
Oh, notes of home

Wide are my wings – cut
High voice that sings – shut
Ride with the kings – blood
"Fly!" turned to "roam…"

Headless and handless
Brav'ry you can't miss
Valor and grandness
Wind made of stone

Count of Time
20. October 2021, 23:25

I bow to you, oh Count of Time
I yield to where I'm stationed
Conceding you're a Lord of mine
I'll finally be patient

Light up with joy

21. October 2021, 00:55

You know, I may not understand
Some things that bring you pleasure
But on your book I'll place my hand
And swear with grace b'yond measure
To see your face light up with joy
Not coy 'bout how you're feeling
Expands my beating heart, oh boy,
That very same you're stealing

Thoughts
21. October 2021, 01:20

Been for hours in bed
Am tired, no doubt
Fatigue deep inside of each bone
But the thoughts in my head
As annoyingly loud
As suitcase wheels on cobblestone

The baggage large that's pulled along
The wheels, on this ground, aren't working
So take I charge and carry strong
But feels and doubts keep lurking

Ooze with Magic

23. October 2021, 13:30

You write "this man does ooze with magic
Lives, breathes, is it, lungs and vein"
Yet you do not see, 'tis tragic,
You yourself do seep the same
Maybe not the kind you're writing
Still a kind deserving note
'Tis exciting and inviting
'Tis a kind on which I dote

Quote credits: Ira Burnstein (unpublished)

Battle Hero

24. October 2021, 01:00

a battle hero, bruised and scarred
yet wears these marks so proudly
from fighting left both soft and hard
copes quietly and loudly
the past in eyes yet joy on lips
still wary yet so friendly
big heart beneath protecting ribs
warm arms that hold so gently

Farewell

26. October 2021, 00:40

I should not write, I do not care
But still, to have 't complete:
"I'll miss you, mourn beyond compare,"
They said with tongue in cheek

Farewell, oh, flare with which you came
Farewell, oh, spell you cast
Not even did this sorry flame
Grant me, oh, one last blast

The Slowest Current
27. October 2021, 00:40

The slowest current moves my boat
No motor, paddle, oar
I'll've writ' a hundred stories
By the time we reach that shore
Why, yes, I like the scenes I pass
So much to prize in store
The land, however, I'm afraid,
I do enjoy much more

Warm Eyes
28. October 2021, 01:11

wish I could have scooted over
arm around your sleepy form
would you have let me
or would you have tensed?
would your eyes 've, when I left, been as warm?

Pour out love
29. October 2021, 00:50

Tell me, please, how do I pour out my love
When your hands aren't open to catch it?
One droplet of rivers unsaid is enough
You step back, shake your head, look away.

Don't you know it'd fill up oceans
If you let our rivers run
Adorations and devotions
Watch it rise from port or bay

Autumn Orange
29. October 2021, 23:05

In autumn orange, warm and bright
I show my hand, you hold it tight
A weight is lifted, lungs are freed
Uncertain, still, where this may lead
In citrus, mint, and ginger air
A step is taken, fine and fair
More safely I will never sink
So let I go of brim and brink
In autumn ev'ning, brisk and dim
I hold your hand, lean back and swim